The Holy Spirit Reveals Satan's Tactics & Strategies In Apostolic Ministries

By

Prophet Anthony Montoya

The Holy Spirit Reveals Satan's Tactics & Strategies In Apostolic Ministries

By

Prophet Anthony Montoya

Copyright @ 2018, All Rights Reserved
Printed in The United States of America

Published By:

ABM Publications
A division of Andrew Bills Ministries Inc.
PO Box 6811, Orange, CA 92863

ISBN: 978-1-931820-89-9

All scripture quotations, unless otherwise indicated are taken from the King James Version of the Bible, Public Domain. Those marked AMP are from the Amplified Bible, copyright @ 1987, The Updated Edition, by the Zondervan Corporation and the Lockman Foundation, and is used by permission. All rights reserved.

DEDICATION

Special thanks to My Mother and Father,

Santiago and Mary,

To my daughter. Alexis Marina Montoya,

And to Lily Avila and Mr. Burns

TABLE OF CONTENTS

	Forward	i
1	Chapter One	1
2	Chapter Two	7
3	Chapter Three	15
4	Chapter Four	23
5	Chapter Five	31
6	Chapter Six	37
7	Chapter Seven	47
	About The Author	55

FORWARD

The Lord has anointed Prophet Anthony Montoya and he is mightily being used of The Holy Spirit with an insightful prophetic word designed for you to experience Yahshua's presence and power, break the bonds of demonic influence, deal with stress and give you victory through Yahshua.

CHAPTER ONE

Saints, Children, Priests of Yah thank you for your acceptance of reading and searching for His truth! I want to thank all of you in every profession you walk in, do not think that the father or Yeshua has forgotten you in any way shape or form. Religion will always try to pin point how you're not being used or what criteria you need to fit in or be compared too. Ignore their ignorance and self-reliance. This means they try or have to fill in the gap of what's hidden within themselves or trying to do the work of the Holy Spirit or Yahweh without him. People involved in ministry are always trying to fill in the Gap without Discernment or patient and without the Will of Yahweh or his Timing. I am going to share with you My Personal Experience of How Demonic Potion Drinks enter into their Hearts, minds, soul and Spirit of Mankind in the Ministry! Most likely like I have stated before in every ministry only 1% of every congregation or group etc. has Keen Discernment or the gift of Discerning of spirits and also to discern the Motive and Intentions of the Heart! I am going to recap two important situations recorded in the Bible that was mentioned before in my other books, so you know how to follow where the Holy Spirit is going with this revelation, knowledge and understanding!

In the Book of Job 1 verse 1 in the land of Uz there lived a man whose name was Job. This man was blameless and upright; he feared God and shunned evil. 2 He had seven sons and three daughters, 3 and he owned seven

thousand sheep, three thousand camels, five hundred yoke of oxen and five hundred donkeys, and had a large number of servants. He was the greatest man among all the people of the East.

4 His sons used to hold feasts in their homes on their birthdays, and they would invite their three sisters to eat and drink with them. Now you notice it states to drink, what kind of drink (Wine Drunkenness) what kind of sort of Witchery was going on in his own house! Let's recap with some scriptures shall we:

Ephesians 5:18 - And be not drunk with wine, wherein is excess; but be filled with the Spirit.

Proverbs 20:1 - Wine [is] a mocker, strong drink [is] raging: and whosoever is deceived thereby is not wise.

Galatians 5:19-21 - 19 the acts of the flesh are obvious: sexual immorality, impurity and debauchery; 20 idolatry and witchcraft; hatred, discord, jealousy, fits of rage, selfish ambition, dissensions, factions 21 and envy; drunkenness, orgies, and the like. I warn you, as I did before, that those who live like this will not inherit the kingdom of God.

Luke 21:34 - And take heed to yourselves, lest at any time your hearts be overcharged with surfeiting, and drunkenness, and cares of this life, and [so] that day come upon you unawares.

Proverbs 23:20 - Be not among winebibbers; among riotous eaters of flesh.

Isaiah 28:7 - But they also have erred through wine, and through strong drink are out of the way; the priest and the prophet have erred through strong drink, they are swallowed up of wine, they are out of the way through strong drink; they err in vision, they stumble [in] judgment.

5 When a period of feasting had run its course, Job would make arrangements for them to be purified. Early in the morning he would sacrifice a burnt offering for each of them, thinking, "Perhaps my children have sinned and cursed God in their hearts." This was Job's regular custom. You notice Job Knew something spiritual and natural was going on in his own house that was a defilement to Yah! Potions and drinks of Demons were entered into the Hearts of his Family just like the story of Noah, I will explain further more on this Subject of Revelation!

1 Corinthians 10:21 you cannot drink the cup of the Lord and the cup of demons too; you cannot have a part in both the Lord's Table and the table of demons.

Spiritual demons know how to mix potions in ministry and enter into your Heart, mind, body, soul and spirit without anyone prophesying to you or even laying hands on you. As long as you agree what's going on in the midst of the meeting or group in your ministry, it can enter within you still! Why or how you say? You have no clue what Discerning of Spirits is and you have no clue or understanding to even see yourself, also discerning the Motive and Intentions of the Heart of the one Speaking! Mostly they don't teach you these things in Ministry do they, when do you ever Consecrate yourself to seek Him Yah Face to Face, it is lifelong everyday 7day a week 24hour commitment, not always seeking ministry, human attention, your will and desires etc.

So you know what was going on in Jobs house, yes even his own wife and children when toxic wine enters the temple of Yah!, yes your body. Yes sleeping with one another gross! Now religion has taught all of us that Satan or God did this to job because fear was in his Heart. Really? His house was in Adultery and Fornication and Orgies continually! Now we all know the father was speaking toward the end about Jobs Pride that was in his Heart! Also, the story of Job explains when he saw himself the inside to have a self-revelation of yourselves. **Job 42:5 I have heard of thee by the hearing of the ear: but now mine eye seethe thee. 6 Wherefore I abhor myself and repent in dust and ashes. He saw himself when he sought the father face to face!**

Most Christians do not want to see themselves because in order to see yourself you need to die to your own self will! Now you're saying wow Job's wife was involved?

Ok let's recap what came out of her mouth, **Matthew 12:34 you brood of vipers, how can you who are evil say** anything good? For the mouth speaks what the heart is full of. **Job 2:9 then said his wife unto him, dost thou still retain thine integrity? Curse God and die.**

Wow Curse God, Blame him for all this and die, Hmmm Saints sounds like His wife is Guilty of something! Wouldn't you rather have your wife be an example of travailing heart before Yah for her own Husband!
Ok now back to **Job 1:6 now there was a day when the sons of God came to present themselves before the LORD, and Satan came also among them.** Saints that means All the Jedi knights were at the table also, just being ironic here, yes even Prophets his Sons were at the Table in the Spirit Realm and they did not Notice the Angel of Light Spirit Lucifer the Angel was sitting amongst them.

7 And the LORD said unto Satan, Whence comest thou? Then Satan answered the LORD, and said, from going to and fro in the earth, and from walking up and down in it.
Only Yeshua knew that Lucifer was there in the midst, because of course Yah created the Gifts and talents! A lot of ministries and leaders have consumed poisoned drinks of mixture within them and still carousing around with their gifts and talents of the anointing!

Yes my beloved Saints the fallen angels are very well trained in Witchery of Potions, ok let me remind you of some Disney Characters that knew how to mix Potions in the spirit! You all notice that in Disney characters the villains every single one of them they walk in a form like of Good character false humility, false character, false Angel of light. These characters knew how to mix Potions in the spirit and natural with strong drink or even with Words! Let me remind you in the beginning Satan spoke to Eve and Deceived her correct! Satan Planted the Seed of Reason within her and she accepted the announcement or words and then bite the apple! What was the outcome she bore a Son Cain! She was even impregnated with a Son in the Natural born of the Devil! All it took was a Word! I will explain more about this as we go on.

CHAPTER TWO

Let's move on shall we saints, **Jude 1:4 for certain men have crept in stealthily [[c]gaining entrance secretly by a side door].** Their doom was predicted long ago, ungodly (impious, profane) persons who pervert the grace (the spiritual blessing and favor) of our God into lawlessness *and* wantonness *and* immorality, and disown *and* deny our sole Master and Lord, Jesus Christ (the Messiah, the Anointed One).

Another version of the scripture states it this way: **4 For there are certain men who have crept in unawares, who were foreordained of old for this condemnation,** Meaning they were ordained through their church or leadership and have been trained, well trained within their hearts to prostitute what they carry, they were never sent or commissioned for the throne of Heaven, they were sent out and ordained, trained because they submitted under them for certain periods of time and then Released by the Hand of Human Intent not The Holy spirit!

Let me remind you in my Personal experience a well anointed Prophet who can see Bullseye within a vessel very sharply whether healing, prophecy in detail, curses iniquities, where it's coming from, deliverance, names, dates etc.! I have Known him for 8years long walking in all the fruits of the spirit but had mixed potions of poison within him. I did warn him several times about what I saw, last but no least I asked him why does he allow certain individuals to preach behind the pulpit in his church when, they do not speak in tongues and also speaks and preaches witchery of carnality of things that were totally not biblical in Purity and Holiness! This is what the words that came out of The Prophets Mouth, He Tithes to me and comes faithfully to my church and submits under me and does whatever I tell him! Last to say this person was ordained within 2years by Human Intent not by the leading of the Holy Spirit! Meaning he paid his way to be ordained!

Ok another Scenario, a much anointed Apostle in a certain city, which I knew the Prophetess who submitted under him. I prophesied to her one day that she was being used by others and ministry leaders of her intercession and gifts for self-gain! She told me that yes it was correct and affirmed by another Prophetess! In her ministry she mentioned that there were several meetings with her Pastor the Apostle certain people who was starting trouble in the congregation and I mentioned to her, is it not the Pastors discretion to remove certain individuals form the ministry!

1 Corinthians 5:12 for what business is it of mine to judge outsiders (non-believers)? Do you not judge those who are within *the church* **[to protect the church as the situation requires]? 13 God** *alone* **sits in judgment on those who are outside [the faith]. REMOVE THE WICKED ONE FROM AMONG YOU [expel him from your church].** This was the words of the Apostle welcome to ministry! Huh, I told her lets speak with some understanding, how you know his intent was to keep them there because of the Tithe and money they bring in.

Later on within the year other vessels I knew personally have attended the ministry and they specifically seen with their own eyes the Apostle tell them several times, I need you all to give a certain amount of money in the offering basket! When some of the individuals went to drop the offering the Apostle would look to see if any money was placed in the offering, then he would even ask how much are you giving?, some would say this is all I have, and he would not use the gift to prophesy over them. He would only prophesy to those that gave the amount he asked for. Also they saw he did not prophesy to you or use the gift if you didn't put any money in the offering!

Saints another experience of another Power Prophet I had to separate myself from, had a powerful healing ministry also! His intentions were sour, as I left his ministry, I was only there for fellowship and also it's a beautiful thing to see people healed. Long story short I caught up with him at a certain event and he asked me to call him and I told him flat out I love you brother and I honor you and respect you, but I will not have anything to do with what's going on in your house! This was his words, no Anthony it has nothing to do with coming to my house, were training those to be sent out to other countries, meaning he has access to ministry doors.

Hello saints was not I speaking of the Book of Jude, those who are trained by their Human Intent. Well you're asking well what's was the Intent? He stated it's an investment if I open ministry doors for you and I send you out and you get a 1,000 dollar offering you give me 10% where ever you go and pick up, he gets 10% in return! Wow is that God like manner or Character or even the Leading of the HOLY SPIRIT, OR THE TIMING OF THE HOLY SPIRIT OR EVEN THE WILL OF YAWEH! No Saints it is not, most people have compromised the word of God and his Holiness.

Now some of you are saying ok well pray for them yes of course, but here is the key cut them off and not entertain their circus acts or even open your hearts to receive their teachings because it has mixed potions. Most of you still except them and unite with them because of the gift and the anointing within them. When you say I love all people and still continue to compromise Gods word your nothing but a fool and a Hypocrite!

Jude 1:8 nevertheless in like manner, these dreamers also corrupt the body, scorn *and* reject authority *and* government, and revile *and* libel *and* scoff at [heavenly] glories (the glorious ones).

10 But these men revile (scoff and sneer at) anything they do not happen to be acquainted with *and* do not understand; and whatever they do understand physically [that which they know by mere instinct], like irrational beasts—by these they corrupt themselves *and* are destroyed (perish).

11 Woe to them! For they have run riotously in the way of Cain, and have abandoned themselves for the sake of

gain [it offers them, following] the error of Balaam, and have perished in rebellion [like that] of Korah!

12 These are hidden reefs (elements of danger) in your love feasts, where they boldly feast sumptuously [carousing together in your midst], without scruples providing for themselves [alone]. They are clouds without water, swept along by the winds; trees, without fruit at the late autumn gathering time—twice (doubly) dead, [lifeless and] plucked up by the roots;

13 Wild waves of the sea, flinging up the foam of their own shame *and* disgrace; wandering stars, for whom the gloom of eternal darkness has been reserved forever.

16 These are inveterate murmurers (grumblers) who complain [of their lot in life], going after their own desires [controlled by their passions]; their talk is boastful *and* arrogant, [and they claim to] admire men's persons *and* pay people flattering compliments to gain advantage.

Here saints let me explain this one to you, the admiring of persons and pay flattering compliments to gain advantage of your (Hearts). When a leader or ministry invites you in and calls you Apostle, Prophet, Deacon, Elder, Pastor, Evangelist gives you some kind of Title in their ministry but never allows you to do anything but just submit under their control you accept it. You accept it because it flatters you to be accepted, your being used and you don't even know it, because your so naïve, ignorant and insecure possibly or even your own will has not yet died or have not come to the end of yourself at all. Why? You seek Ministry and to be used by God, but do not want to wait patiently for what he wants for you in your life.

Let me give you another scenario of a beautiful women character, I ran into her at Costco parking lot, we had a brief talk. Let me remind you she was introduced to the Apostolic order of the bible etc., she receive a new Job or position and she was attending a church well known in a certain city and pretty big church! This church has no apostolic order and filled with compromise and Religious Demons etc. It even has a large youth ministry, anyways I told her just to be careful that's all. These were the words that came out of her mouth, I attend the women's meeting here because this is one of the only days off I have to fellowship and hang out. What a sorry excuse to say I will accept anything of compromise to get attention. Yes sad to say she loves God and his word and prays but accompanied by the wrong peers and ministry! But also what else engulfing in Demonic Potions of witchery also!

Jude 1:17 But you must remember, beloved, the predictions which were made by the apostles (the special messengers) of our Lord Jesus Christ (the Messiah, the Anointed One).

18 They told you beforehand, in the last days (in the end time) there will be scoffers [who seek to gratify their own unholy desires], following after their own ungodly passions.

Now saints let me remind you of your loved ones or best friends what can happened to any of us and sometimes we need to let go and move on without them in our lives and fellowship and heart talks!

Ephesians 4:17 So I tell you this, and insist on it in the Lord, that you must no longer live as the Gentiles do, in the futility of their thinking. 18 They are darkened in their understanding and separated from the life of God because of the ignorance that is in them due to the hardening of their hearts. 19 Having lost all sensitivity, they have given themselves over to sensuality so as to indulge in every kind of impurity, and they are full of greed.

Just because you have known them for 5, 10, 15 years they tell you I love you, act like they are there for you etc. Their hearts have been tainted with War and Drawn Swords for their own Self Gain, truth comes out of their mouth but their Behavior acts differently from what they speak of! I will explain this revelation more in detail saints! You just read their own ignorance have corrupted themselves, they carry now a Judas Spirit! You all know the story of Judas, the Apostle false Humility Kissing you on the cheek, catering to you!

Jude 1:19 It is these who are [agitators] setting up distinctions *and* causing divisions—merely sensual [creatures, carnal, worldly-minded people], devoid of the [Holy] Spirit *and* destitute of any higher spiritual life.

21 Guard *and* keep yourselves in the love of God; expect *and* patiently wait for the mercy of our Lord Jesus Christ (the Messiah)—[which will bring you] unto life eternal.

22 And *refute [so as to] convict some who dispute with you, and* on some have mercy who waver *and* doubt.

23 [Strive to] save others, snatching [them] out of [the] fire; on others take pity [but] with fear, loathing even the garment spotted by the flesh *and* polluted by their sensuality.

CHAPTER THREE

You notice it states to strive to save others, snatching them out of the fire of this mixed potions of witchery. Let me explain something even more profound and hope you get this within your spirit, listen and read attentively and carefully what I'm about to explain to you Saints!

2 Timothy 3:3 but mark this: There will be terrible times in the last days. 2 People will be lovers of themselves, lovers of money, boastful, proud, abusive, disobedient to their parents, ungrateful, unholy, 3 without love, unforgiving, slanderous, without self-control, brutal, not lovers of the good, 4 treacherous, rash, conceited, lovers of pleasure rather than lovers of God— 5 having a form of godliness but denying its power. Have nothing to do with such people.

6 They are the kind who worm their way into homes and gain control over gullible women, who are loaded down with sins and are swayed by all kinds of evil desires, 7 always learning but never able to come to a knowledge of the truth.

Saints it states always learning but never able to come to the knowledge of the truth means the transformation of life giving character and the power within the meat or food or manna, to whatever your hearing or eating.

1 **Corinthians 3:3** you are still [b]worldly [controlled by ordinary impulses, the sinful capacity]. For as long as there is jealousy and strife *and* discord among you, are you not [c]unspiritual, and are you not walking like ordinary men [unchanged by faith]? 4 For when one *of you* says, "I am [a disciple] of Paul," and another, "I am [a disciple] of Apollos," are you not [proving yourselves unchanged, just] *ordinary* people?

5 What then is Apollos? And what is Paul? Just servants through whom you believed [in Christ], even as the Lord appointed to each his task. 6 I planted, Apollos watered, but God [all the while] was causing the growth. 7 So neither is the one who plants nor the one who waters anything, but [only] God who causes the growth.

Everything is giving to the glory of God Yah the father, but let me explain what is introduced here, do not be cloned by irreverent fools who speak truth and give out secrets and mysteries and speak of righteous understand. All of it could be just Head knowledge and no transforming character or power in it at all. Meaning what's missing for or whom the person speaking about righteous understanding, it's called transparency, when there Is no transparency within the vessel, all your getting is head knowledge of this righteous understanding.

Your also receiving several other mixed potions of witchery let me explain, I was speaking with a brother about where he was being taught I told him, I love the revelation and secrets and mysteries of this righteous understanding that is being spoken of. I know what he was speaking of the Prophet or Apostle of the house speaking. Then I started to listen even more carefully, the brother states if you don't have any revelation of secrets or mysteries you're not saved, and stated anyone having righteous understanding must be pure and transparent cause your speaking it and have attained the knowledge of what you're speaking of. First of all to all that Hocus Pocus witchery, that is Religious, just because you don't know any secrets and mysteries that does not mean you're not saved.

Now I was discerning why this coming out of his mouth, the mystery and secret is Christ Crucified and him Resurrecting off the Cross and Believing in him and his name Yeshua. Also it is the Repenting from your sins and asking the Holy Spirit to baptize you with the edification of speaking in tongues. You're asking Yeshua to be lord and savior over you own heart, you then are inviting him within you to guide you and strip you of all things cause your acknowledging you need his help! This you are saved but yes everything is a process of dying to self!

Now just because you're speaking about Righteous understanding and have the knowledge of it does not mean you have come to the end of self! Why you say let me explain?, when the brother was speaking I heard religion coming out of his mouth, then he asked me tell me what revelation did you last teach on?, I said ok, let me give you one, I started to talk than within several seconds he interrupted me several times and would not listen to anything I had to say after he asked me to explain to him what revelation did I last teach on! Hello Saints he carried the spirit of Competition, trying to compete of what I knew, wow where is that coming from. The spirit of competition, boils down to Self, Pride, meaning his mentor the one teaching does not carry The Spirit of Transparency or life of Yeshua speaking of Transformation of Characters its Self-Talking, this is what is being cloned within vessels worldwide.

There getting nothing but puffed up head knowledge of righteous understanding and cloned spirit of the one teaching! How you say? Well its coming out of this brothers mouth two different spirits, the spirit of religion, and competition which carries no transparency in it and no life giving producing fruit at all! All this righteous understanding and secrets and knowledge it not produce transforming character because the one preaching it, has not Died to self or lay down his self-will, or laid down the calling and the gifts and giving all the glory and honor to Yah. The Mentor is doing it all out of self! It's coming out of the servant or student! Just because someone states you need to come to the end of self does not mean they have come to the end of self themselves, because these spirits would not transfer within the students, the spirit of religion and competition spirit which boils down to Self and Pride.

So what's really happening is cloning an idolatry offspring which will produce no fruit when they teach this righteous understanding to others why? Because there was no life or transparency within the vessel teaching it! It was all Self talking ,the seed of the word or revelation carried no weight of any transforming character or Power to come to the Transformation of it, meaning there's no nurture in it no life of Yeshua!, It's all self-talking Saints!

Transparency means you're honest in what you're doing, you admit when you're wrong or you're not hiding the motive and intentions of your heart! You do not carry any Pride at all!

1 Corinthians 3:3 you are still [b]worldly [controlled by ordinary impulses, the sinful capacity]. For as long as there is jealousy and strife *and* discord among you, are you not [c]unspiritual, and are you not walking like ordinary men [unchanged by faith]? 4 For when one *of you* says, "I am [a disciple] of Paul," and another, "I am [a disciple] of Apollos," are you not [proving yourselves unchanged, just] *ordinary* people?

5 What then is Apollos? And what is Paul? Just servants through whom you believed [in Christ], even as the Lord appointed to each his task. 6 I planted, Apollos watered, but God [all the while] was causing the growth. 7 So neither is the one who plants nor the one who waters anything, but [only] God who causes the growth.

19 For the wisdom of this world is foolishness (absurdity, stupidity) before God; for it is written [in Scripture], "[He is] THE ONE WHO CATCHES THE WISE *and* CLEVER IN THEIR CRAFTINESS;" 20 and again, "THE LORD KNOWS THE THOUGHTS of the [humanly] wise, THAT THEY ARE USELESS." 21 So let no one boast in men [about their wisdom, or of having this

or that one as a leader]. Do not make your Mentors and idol!

2 Timothy 3: 10 You, however, know all about my teaching, my way of life, my purpose, faith, patience, love, endurance, 11 persecutions, sufferings—what kinds of things happened to me in Antioch, Iconium and Lystra, the persecutions I endured. Yet the Lord rescued me from all of them. 12 In fact, everyone who wants to live a godly life in Christ Jesus will be persecuted, 13 while evildoers and impostors will go from bad to worse, deceiving and being deceived. 14 But as for you, continue in what you have learned and have become convinced of, because you know those from whom you learned it, 15 and how from infancy you have known the Holy Scriptures, which are able to make you wise for salvation through faith in Christ Jesus. 16 All Scripture is God-breathed and is useful for teaching, rebuking, correcting and training in righteousness, 17 so that the servant of God[a] may be thoroughly equipped for every good work. Training in Righteousness means no hidden motives or agendas, Total transparency!

Let me give you an analogy why or how come or possible another reason you accept compromise. You are of afraid of being persecuted or laughed and mocked amongst those who compromise with one another! You're afraid of being an outcast, a loan shark, not the one they call who doesn't fit in and they point the finger at you and you're the one to blame because they say your to self-righteous and to Holy! They speak and use Parapsychological misinterpretations to describe you. It specifically states you will be Persecuted for the sake of Christ!

2 Corinthians 12:10 that is why for Christs sake I delight in weaknesses, in insults, in hardships, in persecutions, in difficulties for when I am weak I am strong! It states to delight in your persecutions for the Glory of Yah!

To be humiliated for his Honor! Let me give you some illustration since you want to be used by Yah so much, let's recap the story of Isaiah the Prophet!

Isaiah 20:20 In the year that the Tartan [the Assyrian commander in chief] came to Ashdod [in Philistia], when Sargon king of Assyria sent him and he fought against Ashdod and captured it, 2 at that time the LORD** spoke through Isaiah the son of Amoz, saying, "Go, untie the [a]sackcloth from your hips and take your sandals off your feet." And he did so, walking around [b]stripped [to his loincloth] and barefoot. 3 And the L**ORD** said, "Even as My servant Isaiah has walked [c]stripped and barefoot for three years as a sign and forewarning concerning Egypt and Cush (Ethiopia), (Yahweh told his servant to walk naked for three years to show forth thy nakedness of his children Israel, Egypt and Cush) 4 in the same way the king of Assyria will lead away the Egyptian captives and the Cushite exiles, young and old, stripped and barefoot, even with buttocks uncovered—to the [d]shame of Egypt. 5 Then they will be dismayed and ashamed because of Cush their hope and Egypt their boast. 6 So the inhabitants of this coastland [the Israelites and their**

neighbors] will say in that day, 'Look what has happened to those in whom we hoped *and* trusted and to whom we fled for help to be spared from the king of Assyria! But we, how will we escape [captivity and exile]?'"

It is speaking of those you put your hope and trust in, to be very Keen and careful who you share your hearts with and trust! Also Yahweh used Isaiah in complete Humiliation for the sake of Yahs kingdom! Mostly everyone wants to agree with the majority, ministry, television, radio etc. The life and calling as a Nazarite it to risk a life of Torment and derision for the sake of Mankind and Yahs Kingdom!

CHAPTER FOUR

Let me give you another scenario, I recently in 2015, separated myself from another brother Prophet/Evangelist and Sister Prophetess. Did it not state in his word its ok to correct and rebuke one another in love and with careful instructions! Well one of the brother and sister I knew for about 10 years or so, very good hearted and transparent children.

The brother started having meetings in his home, I was called to minister and it went well. The brother wanted to continue to have meetings once a month, and of course he is lead to whatever he wishes between him and the father! I told him what I was picking up in the spirit that he was trying to promote himself and Ministry was not for him at all at this point in time. I told him the father wants to deliver you from self completely and there is no ministry for you right now, I said it out of love.

The brother started to come against me with words and psychological interpretations of how I'm not the same anymore or I've changed etc. Basically he did not like the rebuke in any way. Several times in the last 12 months when we met up we both smelled a strong Toxic drink of wine that was foul and a huge stench to our nostrils! The last time we smelled it together was at his house after the first meeting service he held, yes the Prophet. I asked the Holy Spirit what it was, Holy Spirit said he has strong toxic poison of religion deeply rooted within him and it rises like a huge tree! He is not to be preaching or Prophesying or using his gifts. I told him your joy does not come from your gift, it's supposed to come from Yeshua alone and only him! He stated well of course my joy comes from the gift when God uses me to speak to someone. Meaning he admitted he worships the gift more than the giver!

That's when I just ignored him and didn't say anything, I knew he was in denial about a certain matter within him. I did tell him you're imparting poison and mixture within other vessels because it's inside you still and to stop the ministry. He did not take it very well at all. Within a week I received a photograph of the sister we both knew together of her flipping me off with the middle finger! I thought it was just a joke because were all human, holy spirit said that is both of them telling you I don't need your friendship anymore, if you're not going to be part of my compromising ministry! Meaning they both have not died to their wills, they have made a decision in their hearts to walk out of the will of Yah and push Ministry without the leading of the Holy Spirit on their own with their gifts and talents!

Now mind you the Prophetess that gave me the middle finger, two months ago I was fooled and manipulated to give her $300 dollars for her and her children in need, now she is very well gifted in the anointing as a great Seer anointing! Yes she even turned her back on me after 10years of fellowship, and after I lend her $300 dollars just two months prior to the situation. Holy spirit lead me to cut them off completely, what I'm trying to illustrate to you

Saints these children are Mixing Potions like in a Laboratory and mixture of Poison spiritually and naturally to make anything work and 50% of it is self-will and 50% is in Self Denial! Why you say? Their intention is Seeking Ministry work without the Approval or Leading of the Holy Spirit and Timing of Yah! Well also they are tired of waiting for so long for whatever there searching for, but the answer and redemption of it all, they need to take heed to the instructions Yahweh's gives us and Obey and not run ahead of him or fall back behind him, but be in his perfect divine will, we need to Die to Self Will complete!

Let me tell you this it is a frightening experience to die to self-will, when the Baptism of Fire the Holy Spirit lays us on the surgery table he uses a scalpel or a Sword to receive a transformed Heart! There are three Baptism of Death you go through! Welcome to Yahweh's Kingdom! Well let me put it this way imaging he told you to stop going out, stop drinking, stop hanging around certain meetings, don't go out so much. Stay in your room for months, days, weeks, maybe several years until he does a certain work within you.

Well I mean of course you go to eat and work and run erons still but mostly what I just mentioned. You probably would pull your hair right out, well of course Moses was sent to the Wilderness the Desert for some time correct! This is the time of Self Emptying and Dying to self-will and it's frightening! I can tell you within the end it's so Glorious and Peaceful when you're Transformed and 10times better living and sleeping!

Let me give you another Scenario of the Cup of Demons table! Several years ago I was in involved in another ministry beautiful good Hearted Woman and her ministry. They tried to sit me down and bow down and submit to their own will, now mind you they even gave me money every Saturday 100$ or so.

They would never let me preach or let me utilize what God has given me. Oh well I was humbled just to be part of the Ministry, well long story short I told the Leadership I don't believe in Tithing, I believe in Sacrifice in all things as long it's all heart and the motive and intentions of the heart are pure. I did tell her well if Yahweh said to Tithe to certain ministries or Leadership that's fine, But to say if you Don't Tithe your cursed is witchcraft!

So one time she used me to speak to her ministry, I gave a small interpretation on Sacrifice and it's not in how much you Tithe, everything you do is Sacrifice and lead by the Holy spirit and Pure Heart! After I was finished, well within few minutes I was interrupted by one of her Jezebel spirit friends she knew for 20years. She even admitted she has a controlling spirit, and still she listened to her advice to cut me off from speaking and to sit down. The minute I stop speaking, no one layed hands on me or even spoke to me with any words at all, I felt a strong toxic drink enter my spirit, like if I took a Cup and Drin ked it! It felt so weird, the spirit of influence entered my spirit, not the good influence the witchery Influential spirit. I was shocked, and also the woman said right after she grabbed the microphone she said you see Anthony Believes in Tithe and Offering, which I never said or stated! She came up to me after the service and told me she picked up $2700 her dollars that day, and out of 7years of her ministry she never received more than $500 dollars.

She used and prostituted me in the ministry, that day I went home and cried out to the father not to Judge me, he stated don't worry I'm teaching you, and now you can discern what goes on in Ministry worldwide. Even when you're in the midst or part of the congregation these Cup of Demonic potions enters the children's or saints spirits! Yes they don't even know it themselves.

Later on I Questioned the Woman Minister and caught her in several lies, and would not tell the truth. I said oh no another Jezebel controlling spirit! Even though she has a great good side to her, yes we are to look at Gods children through Yeshuas Eyes, but with Strong discernment to discern the Motive and intentions of the Heart! Her intention was to destroy me and my Joy to keep me in bondage because she was in bondage herself even though she had lots of Money and big ministry!

A prophetess I knew was called in for a meeting, one who Intercedes 4to6 hours a day and has strong discernment! She prophesied to the Woman and said and I Quote! These are the words that were spoken over her, the spirit and Angel of Yahs wrath, judgement and rebuke is upon your head, you do what I tell you what to do and stop controlling the ministry, I tell you who preaches and teaches.

Two years later she lost half her ministry, lost a church gathering building and now in 2016 she is dealing with Throat cancer and has moved and transferred to her Heart the cancer! She lost numerous amounts of blood and hospitalized for three days! Yes we all need to take head to Yahweh's instructions and obey his will!

Psalms 55:12 If an enemy were insulting me, I could endure it; if a foe were rising against me, I could hide. 13 But it is you, a man like myself, my companion, my close friend, 14 with whom I once enjoyed sweet fellowship at the house of God, as we walked about among the worshipers.

20 My companion attacks his friends; he violates his covenant. 21 His talk is smooth as butter, yet war is in his heart; his words are more soothing than oil, yet they are drawn swords.

It specifically states when the heart has turned into sour ignorance or even hard hearted it will still, kill and destroy anyone that's close to them because they are bound within themselves, they play a convincing role like everything is ok!

It specifically states his talk is as smooth as butter, the anointing the gift, the prophecies, the teaching etc., but war was in his Heart (Self and Pride No Transparency) his words are more soothing than oil (His calling, Position, Title, His ministry etc.) yet they are drawn swords (Competing spirit of Self will). From charab; drought; also a cutting instrument (from its destructive effect), as a knife, sword, or other sharp implement -- axe, dagger, knife, mattock, sword, tool. In Hebrew sword also means a Tool, a tool is utilized for working or experimenting! Is it being used for self-gain?

Butter in Hebrew curd-like, smooth, unctuous, and hypocritical...

a. words of flattery (fig.) machămâ'âh. Soothing in Hebrew means nîychôach, nîychôach **Brown-Driver-Briggs' Definition**
1. Soothing, quieting, tranquillizing. Tranquillizing you means to sedate you to a lower level of consciousness, to trap you , make you unaware of my devices

It means his words or his tools are more soothing than oil, meaning the Angel of light character seduces you in an incomprehensible way you cannot discern if you're not well trained in the Spirit!

CHAPTER FIVE

Saints let me give you another story in the bible where these demons entered the Children of Yah!

Genesis 49: Then Jacob called for his sons and said, "Assemble yourselves [around me] that I may tell you what will happen to you *and* **your descendants** [a]**in the days to come.** ²**"Gather together and hear, O sons of Jacob; and listen to Israel (Jacob) your father.**

3

"Reuben, you are my [b]**firstborn; my might, the beginning of my strength** *and* **vigor, Preeminent in dignity and preeminent in power [that should have been your birthright].** ⁴**"But unstable** *and* **reckless** *and* **boiling over like water [in sinful lust], you shall** [c]**not excel** *or* **have the preeminence [of the firstborn], because you went up to your father's bed [with Bilhah]; you defiled it—he went up to my couch. Same thing went on in Jacobs house Fornication, adultery and sleeping with family members! Orgies!**

5

"Simeon and Levi are brothers [equally headstrong, deceitful, vindictive, and cruel]; their swords are weapons of violence *and* **revenge.** ⁶**"O my soul, do not come into their secret council; Let not my glory (honor) be united with their assembly [for I knew nothing of their plot];**

Here is a Key nugget when you enter into a ministry meeting, crusade, church gathering etc. Speak these words over you "O my soul, do not come into their secret council: (Their motive and intentions of their heart, the secret agenda, the demonic potions of spirit, so it does not transfer within you) Let not my glory (Honor) be united with their assembly (for I knew nothing of their plot).

This means just what It says, let not my spirit be entertained with (Angel of Light spirit) their wicked assembly! Also let not your soul compromise and agree with their agenda! Meaning when you're in the midst and you can see what they're doing, even though you don't agree with it and what they believe or teach or even the compromise and you're not involved in any way. You still can have demonic cups and drinks enter your spirit because you still attend the gathering on a normal basis it becomes an agreement, they will probably use you some kind of way to get you to agree somehow by just a gesture or with words and possible allow you speak for a brief moment and twist it on you!

Let me clarify it more simply, (Let not my soul enter in their secret council, nor let my glory unite in their wicked assembly) some other bibles descriptions! Some you say why are these attacks coming or entering you, possibly you are in your wrong position in your walk of life. Meaning some of you are in ministry and Yahweh never sent you out to field ministry, some of you are in the wrong place at the wrong time. Some of you are just to be in intercession for a time being, waiting on God to endue you with power or waiting till he sends you out. Some of you have accepted your own will what you want and not his will! Gods way not yours!

Saints let me give you some understanding of more Revelation, and the spirit of Timing. Spiritual timing, everything has to do with Spiritual timing! Let me give you a Sweet Revelation, Adam and Eve, in the Garden was the Tree of Life correct!

Genesis 2:8 The LORD God planted a garden toward the east, in Eden; and there He placed the man whom He had formed. 9 Out of the ground the LORD God caused to grow every tree that is pleasing to the sight and good for food; the tree of life also in the midst of the garden, and the tree of the knowledge of good and evil. 10 Now a river flowed out of Eden to water the garden; and from there it divided and became four rivers....

Yeshua is the Tree of life, the tree of the Life and the tree of knowledge of good and evil were of the same Tree. According to Hebrew theory, Yeshua is the Tree of Life, Right of the tree was Knowledge of Good fruit (Function) (the middle is Yeshua Timing) The Left side was Evil (Dysfunction)!

Let me Clarify this scenario, When Yeshua Died on the Cross, **Luke 23:39 one of the criminals who had been hanged [on a cross beside Him] kept hurling abuse at Him, saying, "Are you not the Christ? Save yourself and us [from death]!" 40 But the other one rebuked him, saying, "Do you not even fear God, since you are under the same sentence of condemnation? 41 We are suffering justly, because we are getting what we deserve for what we** have done; but this Man has done nothing wrong." 42 And he was saying, "Jesus, [please] remember me when you come into your kingdom!" 43 Jesus said to him, "I assure you and most solemnly say to you, today you will be with me in [me] Paradise."

One side was Good, the other Evil! **John 19:18 There they crucified Him, and with Him two others, one on each side, with Jesus in the middle.**

Yeshua is the In between the middle, the tree of Life (Character, Proper balance function, Alignment when your rooted and grounded in Christ Yeshua). Also I mention to you Timing, Eve was originally created to birth Christ in the Garden, The tree resembled Christ alone! When Lucifer came to Disrupt Eve's birthing, just by a word or seed or sperm of impregnation by spoken words, it caused her DNA to Malfunction improperly! She was originally created to birth Yeshua into the earth! To Restore, Redeem and bring Restitution to all things.

Adam and eve were not the First Creation. Satan came to cause wrong or create wrong or disrupt the Timing of Yah! When you walk out of the Timing of the Holy Spirit, you can miss it! Miss what? I don't know, because each individual has its own course, but we our destiny and courses of purpose and life can be altered drastically walking out of the Timing of the Holy Spirit!

Saints ponder on this for a brief moment, why do you think in Ministry worldwide, everyone gets prayer all the time, always wanting a prophetic word or some stronghold to be broken, because in Ministry you have what you call a racing spirit, doing the work of the ministry without the Leading of the Holy spirit! You're just moving in your gift, not being led by the spirit, there is a difference between gifts and talents and the Orchestration and leading of the Power of the Holy Spirit!

Romans 8:14 for those who are led by the Spirit of God are the children of God. This scripture doesn't mean being led by your gifts and talents, using them like a light switch, turning it on and off whenever you want! The bible teaches the Gifts and callings or without repentance!

Oh ok let's Clarify a Scripture, **Joshua 6: Now Jericho [a fortified city with high walls] was tightly closed because [of the people's fear] of the sons of Israel; no one went out or came in. 2 The Lord said to Joshua, "See, I have given Jericho into your hand, with its king and the mighty warriors. 3 Now you shall march around the city, all the men of war circling the city once. You shall do this [once each day] for six days. 4 Also, seven priests shall carry seven trumpets [made] of rams' horns ahead of the ark; then on the seventh day you shall march around the city seven times, and the priests shall blow the trumpets.**

5 When they make a long blast with the ram's horn, and when you hear the sound of the trumpet, all the people shall cry out with a great shout (battle cry); and the wall of the city will fall down in its place, and the people shall go up, each man [going] straight ahead [climbing over the rubble]." Yahweh spoke to Joshua to do things in proper timing hello! 10 But Joshua commanded the people, "You shall not shout [the battle cry] nor let your voice be heard nor let a word come out of your mouth, until the day I tell

you to shout. Then you shall shout!" **11 So Joshua had the ark of the Lord taken around the city [on the first day], circling it once; then they came back into the camp and spent the night in the camp.**

Joshua stated do not shout until I tell you too! **15 Then on the seventh day they got up early at daybreak and marched around the city in the same way seven times; only on that day they marched around the city [a]seven times. 16 And the seventh time, when the priests had blown the trumpets, Joshua said to the people, "Shout! For the Lord has given you the city.**

Hello Saints, the ministry is not walking in Conquering Mode due to miss firing or out of the Timing of the Leading of the Holy Spirit! When you walk in the Timing of the Leading of the Holy Spirit, you walk in full dominion! Some people or Greek mindset set say well God is a God of the Now! Everything is Now, so there is something wrong or something were missing, that's all called Religion, the answer is Proper Timing! If they did not walk in Proper timing they would have never conquered the city! It states in the bible we are more than Conquers through Christ Yahushua, only when you walk in Proper spiritual timing, obedience and obey his instructions also! **Joshua 6: 20 So the people shouted [the battle cry], and the priests blew the trumpets. When the people heard the sound of the trumpet, they raised a great shout and the wall [of Jericho] fell down, so that the sons of Israel went up into the city, every man straight ahead [climbing over the rubble], and they overthrew the city.**

CHAPTER SIX

Let me give you another form of Revelation, The tree of life is Yeshua, when you're rooted and grounded in Purity, also when the Motive and Intentions of the Heart are Pure! Middle, The tree of life Purity Christ within you the hope of Glory, left side Motive, Right side intention. Dying to self, laying down your will and also dying to your own self will! What did Yeshua say, not my will be done but your will be done Father!

Revelation 2:7 whoever has ears, let them hear what the Spirit says to the churches. To the one who is victorious, I will give the right to eat from the tree of life, which is in the paradise of God.

Tree of Life is Yeshua himself, of creation and Yahs heart! Paradise is Torah (Secrets and Mysteries). **Isaiah 46:10 I make known the end from the beginning, from ancient times, what is still to come?** I say, 'My purpose will stand, and I will do all that I please.' It speaks of things still to come, from ancient times which was not known or revealed!

Isaiah 45:3 I will give you hidden treasures, riches stored in secret places, so that you may know that I am the Lord, the God of Israel, who summons you by name. Other bible interpretation "I will give you the treasures of darkness [the hoarded treasures]

And the hidden riches of secret places, I form the light and create darkness, I bring prosperity and create disaster; I, the Lord, do all these things. The Tree resembles character and function still, He forms Light (Secret something that is Revealed, creator of Darkness Mysteries unknown that has not been revealed yet)! He brings Prosperity (Good) and Create Disaster Evil). **1 Corinthians 15:8 last of all, as though I had been born at the wrong time, I also saw him!** Paul the Apostle by the spirit saw the Future and wanted to be in this Time and generation now! He specifically states I am a man born out of the wrong time, that's why he made that statement!

Let me give you also miscalculated scripture or misinterpretation of scripture, this revelation is also spoken of in my other books!

Malachi 3: 8 "Will a man rob God? Yet you are robbing me! But you say, 'In what way have we robbed you?' In tithes and offerings [you have withheld]. 9 You are cursed with a curse, for you are robbing me, this whole nation!

Tithe means reverence portion of a whole (Your whole Heart) offering means living your life as a sacrificial lamb unto him, by dying to self, laying down your self will and dying to your self will! Yes this means also your repentance! Turning from your wicked ways, Tithes, Motive and Intentions of your Heart! Offerings your gifts and talents, are they being used to glorify God Yahweh or for your self-gain!

Saints let's move on **1 Corinthians 2: [9] However, as it is written: "What no eye has seen, what no ear has heard, and what no human mind has conceived"**[b]—**the things**

God has prepared for those who love him—[10] these are the things God has revealed to us by his Spirit. The Spirit searches all things, even the deep things of God.

Let me give you another Spirit led Revelation, let me remind you Revelation comes in many forms. The tree in the Garden of Eden was a Tree of Knowledge and Power, The father told Adam and Eve not to eat of it and you will surely die!

Now Ezekiel 28:4 With your own wisdom and with your own understanding you have gotten you riches and power and have brought gold and silver into your treasuries; 5 By your great wisdom and by your traffic (Trading) you have increased your riches and power, and your heart is proud and lifted up because of your wealth; the bible was speaking to The Prince of Tyre. Trafficking has to do with illegal trading.

12 Son of man, take up a lamentation over the king of Tyre and say to him, thus says the Lord God: You are the full measure and pattern of exactness [giving the finishing touch to all that constitutes completeness], full of wisdom and perfect in beauty.

13 You were in [a] Eden, the garden of God; every precious stone was your covering, the carnelian, topaz, jasper, chrysotile, beryl, onyx, sapphire, carbuncle, and emerald; and your settings and your sockets and engravings were wrought in gold. On the day that you were created they were prepared.

14 You were the anointed cherub that covers with overshadowing [wings], and I set you so. You were upon

the holy mountain of God; you walked up and down in the midst of the stones of fire [like the paved work of gleaming sapphire stone upon which the God of Israel walked on Mount Sinai].

15 You were blameless in your ways from the day you were created until iniquity and guilt were found in you.

16 Through the abundance of your commerce (Trade) you were filled with lawlessness and violence, and you sinned; therefore I cast you out as a profane thing from the mountain of God and the guardian cherub drove you out from the midst of the stones of fire.

17 Your heart was proud and lifted up because of your beauty; you corrupted your wisdom for the sake of your splendor. I cast you to the ground; I lay you before kings that they might gaze at you.

18 You have profaned your sanctuaries by the multitude of your iniquities and the enormity of your guilt, by the unrighteousness of your trade. Therefore I have brought forth a fire from your midst; it has consumed you, and I have reduced you to ashes upon the earth in the sight of all who looked at you. You notice it stated my unrighteous trade, now let's ponder on this revelation. How Did Satan deceive 1/3 of the angels of heaven? Satan wanted to increase His territory even the more and become bigger and more Knowledge able. So Satan possibly ate of the tree of Knowledge and Power without the Fathers Permission!

Satan committed Treason by eating or obtaining something that was not rightfully granted by God! He traded something in return for it, even with the 1/3 of the angels. There was nothing wrong with the tree, it all has to do with an act of Reverence and Obedience and Acknowledge who you're Father and creator is! Satan moves in cycles, circles and patterns upon human souls. He was first to eat of the tree, it was a test of loyalty. Hebrew word for Trade is Rekellah Merchandise, traffic, trade. Hebrew word Rakal or Bakal (To go about). There is trading in the Heavens! This has to do with are you Prostituting yourself for wrong intentions or impure motives and agendas. Satan puts a wage on your Royalty Rights.

Job 2: 2 again there was a day when the sons of God [the angels] came to present themselves before the Lord, and Satan (the adversary and the accuser) came also among them to present himself before the Lord.

2 And the Lord said to Satan, from where do you come? And Satan (the adversary and the accuser) answered the Lord, from going to and fro on the earth and from walking up and down on it.

You notice it states to and fro, Satan and his kingdom servants are looking for those he can trade with unrighteous for his expansion of his Kingdom, also in apostolic ministry. **You cannot drink the cup of the Lord and the cup of demons too; you cannot have a part in both the Lord's Table and the table of demons. 1 Corinthians 10:21.**

It's been happening in the ministry because leaders have drank these potions within them, this unrighteous trade and teaches others how to maneuver in it!

1 Samuel 9: ...8 The servant answered Saul again and said, "Behold, I have in my hand a fourth of a shekel of silver; I will give it to the man of God and he will tell us our way." 9 (Formerly in Israel, when a man went to inquire of God, he used to say, "Come, and let us go to the seer"; for he who is called a prophet now was formerly called a seer.)

It is righteous to honor the Prophet or Apostle for clarity, but when a Leader puts a Price and specific amount on his lips that's called Trafficking or trading the gift and anointing and his word! It needs to come from the heart of the Person giving it! Meaning the gift of Prophecy for specific amount and say God Said!

Numbers 21: 17 Then Israel sang this song: "Spring up, O well! Sing about it,

18 about the well that the princes dug, that the nobles of the people sank— the nobles with scepters and staffs." In a place of famine Israel sang, praised God and worshipped him for the increase, favor and Multiplication in the midst of desperateness and desire!

Many of you have been unrighteous trading or trafficking because of insecurity issues or loneliness or some other unrighteous reasons!

Genesis 14: 21 the king of Sodom said to Abram, "Give me the people and keep the goods for yourself."22 But Abram said to the king of Sodom, "With raised hand I have sworn an oath to the Lord, God Most High, Creator of heaven and earth, 23 that I will accept nothing belonging to you, not even a thread or the strap of a sandal, so that you will never be able to say, 'I made

Abram rich.' 24 I will accept nothing but what my men have eaten and the share that belongs to the men who went with me—to Aner, Eshkol and Mamre. Let them have their share." King of Sodom means Evil one, Satan also came as an angel of light Spirit to trade with Abraham and Abraham refused to trade with him.

Ezekiel 16:49 "'now this was the sin of your sister Sodom: She and her daughters were arrogant, overfed and unconcerned; they did not help the poor and needy. God is telling the people to feed and aid the poor! Isaiah 1:17 Learn to do right; seek justice. Defend the oppressed. [A]Take up the cause of the fatherless, plead the case of the widow. 23 Your rulers are rebels, partners with thieves; they all love bribes and chase after gifts. They do not defend the cause of the fatherless; the widow's case does not come before them.

James 1:27 27 Religion that God our Father accepts as pure and faultless is this: to look after orphans and widows in their distress and to keep oneself from being polluted by the world.

Why does not the body of Christ help those people who are sitting right next to them in church? **Revelation 3:18 I counsel you to buy from me gold refined in the fire, so you can become rich; and white clothes to wear, so you can cover your shameful nakedness; and salve to put on your eyes, so you can see.** He wants us to put on Spiritual righteous eyes of understanding.

Isaiah 54: 12 And I will make your windows and pinnacles of [sparkling] agates or rubies, and your gates of [shining]

carbuncles, and all your walls [of your enclosures] of precious stones.

Hebrew word for agate shebo: (a precious stone) perhaps agate, from an unused root (probably identical with that of shabah through the idea of subdivision into flashes or streamers (compare shabiyb) meaning to flame; a gem (from its sparkle), probably the agate -- agate. He wants us to be on Fire for him and also our exposure within us To Flame to burn out everything even within our midst to become holy and pure! In verse 12 he is speaking of Spiritual Timing, windows are considered to see or open visually in the spirit. He wants us to give up our Human timing and receive his Spiritual Timing!

Timing is also Unity in the Spirit! He wants us to be in proper balance in spiritual timing and human proper timing as well! What I mean is to give up our human self-will timing just to go about what we want and moved by our emotions and feelings which is not good!.

How are rubies are formed(The commonly held belief amongst geologists is that rubies are formed by tectonic plates smashing together – as did the India and Asia plates when the Himalayan mountains were formed around 50 million years ago – forcing limestone deposits deep into the earth where intense heat and pressure metamorphosed the limestone into sparkly marble. At the same time, molten granite bubbled up into the marble and removed the silica but left behind the aluminum through a process called metasomatism. It was over time and intense Heat of magma! Spiritual timing can alter events with the natural instantaneously that beats physics laws and comprehension of the unknown!

If you all seen the Movie the Matrix Neo and his clan went to rescue and what they needed was the Key maker! One part of the movie they had to enter into a building that had many doors, the Key maker stated we have to open a certain Door at the Right time, if not all is lost forever! You can miss it without Spiritual timing! Yes also in the movie you notice doors open to certain pathways but when they shut and reopen at wrong times it leads to distances and pathways that need to be redirected to its right path!

CHAPTER SEVEN

Ecclesiastes 3 Speaks about there is a time for everything hello! The human religious spirit with their gifts prophecy according to the atmosphere of the natural on the natural occurrences and seasons. Which is to say it is totally different from the Timing of the Holy Spirit and the Orchestration of the spirit of Yah! There is a Spirit of Comparing and Competition that's involved in this Apostolic Ministry. Trying to see what's being said in the spirit by soulish power and gift!

2 Corinthians 10:12 Not that we dare to classify or compare ourselves with some of those who are commending themselves. But when they measure themselves by one another and compare themselves with one another, they are without understanding. There is what you call a Timing Belt of Heaven which is Spiritual Timing!

John 6:26 Jesus answered, "Very truly I tell you, you are looking for me, not because you saw the signs I performed but because you ate the loaves and had your fill. 27 Do not work for food that spoils, but for food that endures to eternal life, which the Son of Man will give you. For on him God the Father has placed his seal of approval."

Work in Greek means Ergazomai means to make gain by trading or business! In heaven when you plead with him

Yah wants to know what are you trading or sacrificing for him or giving up for His intimacy and to fall in love with him! Ok let me clarify and specifically introduce to you some Key elements of what I speak of about Trading in the spirit and heavens as well as the Natural which you do not know about or if you have studied law!

You notice Isaiah 54:12 talking about agates or gate, we all know that Yeshua when he died and Resurrected he went to Hell the gates and took the keys of Life and Death from Satan! Correct? Ok, now this means he took the keys of The Timing of Humans only to live 120 years and also the timings of natural cycles and patterns he uses for curses on mankind kind through bloodlines and other avenues to steal your Royalty rights.

The Key maker is Yahushua, Holy spirit and Yahweh there all one, **Isaiah 22: I will place on his shoulder the key to the house of David; what he opens no one can shut, and what he shuts no one can open.**

Alright let's go Deeper in the spirit, there is always a Gatekeeper involved also, that could be an ungodly soul tie, a leader, or even the Adversary Satan. Gatekeeper means Treasury or Treasurer someone who sifts or steals or causes division or attack force ably to alter you Royalty rights. Just like what Judas the Gatekeeper, the Treasurer, this is even included in the Heavens and in the Natural Court room, let me Explain!

Isaiah 43: 26 Put Me in remembrance [remind me of your merits]; let us plead and argue together. Set forth your case, that you may be justified (proved right) He is asking you what are you trading in the spirit, are you given him his time with you, are you dying to self, dying to your own will, are you practicing and applying the fruits of the spirit. Now you know there is the Principality rulers in the Heavens Satan battling your Prayers and Petitions the Gatekeeper.

Jeremiah 12:1 you are always righteous, Lord, when I bring a case before you. Yet I would speak with you about your justice: Isaiah 41:21 "Present your case," says the Lord. "Set forth your arguments," says Jacob's King.

Now at this moment Satan is accusing you of anything and everything no matter what, repent and plead the blood of Repentance every time you pray! Now let's get into the trading in the Natural at a Court room, when you receive a Traffic ticket you're summoned to court. Which you don't know there is trading and Business involved which you may or may not know about. It is illegal for Cops to give you a traffic citation, why you say, when you're charged with a fine that makes the cop a third party which makes him a Tax Collector and he has violated Four Federal Laws.

Anyhow your traffic ticket comes with a cussip number and bond on that ticket and has a price on it trading in Wall Street yes money is involved on every case! Also when you're pleading your case before the judge, the judge is getting 7 to 10 percent on your traffic citation in his retirement fund! According to Judicial cannon number 7 judges are not allowed to collect any interest in court because there already paid by the state. Well there you go there is your Gatekeeper a mysterious familiar spirit or unrighteous trade that's already delegated without your

Knowledge! There you go trading and business.

So what I'm trying to clarify to you is Spiritual Timing has the Specific Fire to untrade and reveres all things!

Over a Year or Two Years ago Prophet Joe Rivera from Puerto Rico Prophesied to me and said you have asked the Holy spirit to give you and understand and move in Spiritual Timing, I was blown away and I said Yes! Now Saints according to Scientific intelligence we all have a twofold DNA strand one from our father and mothers chromosomes.

There is a revelation to connect to a Third String DNA which is Yahushua. In the book of **Acts chap 20: [7]And on the first day of the week, when we were assembled together to break bread [[a]the Lord's Supper], Paul discoursed with them, intending to leave the next morning; and he kept on with his message until midnight.**

[8] Now there were numerous lights in the upper room where we were assembled,

[9] And there was a young man named Eutychus sitting in the window. He was borne down with deep sleep as Paul kept on talking still longer, and [finally] completely overcome by sleep, he fell down from the third story and was picked up dead.

[10] But Paul went down and bent over him and embraced him, saying, make no ado; his life is within him.

[11] When Paul had gone back upstairs and had broken bread and eaten [with them], and after he had talked confidentially *and* communed with them for a

considerable time—until daybreak [in fact]—he departed.

¹² They took the youth home alive, and were not a little comforted *and* cheered *and* refreshed *and* encouraged.

You noticed Paul the Apostle took communion twice. In ministry before he stared preaching he took communion and then after a man fell out the window and died and Paul went down resurrected the body came back up and took communion again before he started preaching again. Now there is some great significance in this scenario in the bible. It is a divine revelation and mystery unveiling. It reconnects us to our fathers DNA chromosomes in heaven the three fold Cord of Immortality Power!

In most recent ministry I don't understand why they don't take communion when they assemble. One incident we were in a house and we all took communion before a service ministry meeting and all our eyes were closed, one lady fell out after she took communion and was delivered. All spirits that were attached to her were sent back to the pit of hell. We don't think she was even saved. When Yahushua died on the cross one of the men told Christ to remember him and Yeshua told him this day you will be with me in Paradise! Now I believe that man took communion spiritually, For his words says those who eat of my body, which is sacrificial and eating his words of the Torah and believe, and drink his blood, which is repentance shall live forever.

So that man eat his words and believed and sacrificially vouched for Christ that he was the King of Kings, and he did no wrong but stated we deserve this punishment, then repented in his Heart! That was a form of communion! That threefold DNA of Spiritual Timing was spoken of at the Perfect moment at the right place at the right Time!

The Three fold DNA is Timing of Yah. **Philippians 3: [9] And that I may [actually] be found *and* known as in Him, not having any [self-achieved] righteousness that can be called my own, based on my obedience to the Law's demands (ritualistic uprightness and supposed right standing with God thus acquired), but possessing that [genuine righteousness] which comes through faith in Christ (the Anointed One), the [truly] right standing with God, which comes from God by [saving] faith.**

[10] [For my determined purpose is] that I may know Him [that I may progressively become more deeply and intimately acquainted with Him, perceiving and recognizing and understanding the wonders of His Person more strongly and more clearly], and that I may in that same way come to know the power outflowing from His resurrection [[b]which it exerts over believers], and that I may so share His sufferings as to be continually transformed [in spirit into His likeness even] to His death, [in the hope]

To know him in me as his character of transformation that we may decrease and him increase within me but to complete death to self and die to self-will! Now I spoke in the beginning of this book about Unforbidden Knowledge, or forbidden, you're not allowed to access or eat of certain food. Now yes Revelation is wonderful but if your character is not in the right alignment it becomes unforbidden fruit! Paul in the bible speaks of only feeding or sucking on milk, which immaturity of character and stated I cannot feed you Meat, which is revelation, because they were too immature to eat of it! The body of Christ is feeding and obtaining unforbidden knowledge in the spirit by their own gifts and soul power and feeding it to immature Saints! Unforbidden knowledge is also forbidden when a speaker even a Prophet or Apostle has no Transparency within, them it is forbidden to speak of it when there out of alignment also! You're asking how meaning there agenda is for self-gain, Pride, no life nurturing love of Transparency, their motive and intentions of their heart is not Pure!

You will notice demonic potions within vessels who speak out of competing sprit or comparing religiously out of character that is a reason you should not go to their gathering even if its great Hebrew revelation, the words they speak carry no life or transparency of Purity!

This is what most Saints in ministry cannot fathom or understand at all! How can you walk out of the Spiritual timing of Yah? Ignorance, you cannot feed Revelation to People who Accept Ignorance or are ignorant within themselves! Satan or your own self loves to speak to your own Reasoning! Also there is a General demonic spirit called the Psycho spirit that ministers transfers their souls within you, the spirit of Psychology is not the general it's the Psycho spirit. The demonic spirit comes along like an umbilical cord just like a baby born and attached to its mother, Most Christians cannot break away for friends, family, ungodly people, ministry, congregations, soul ties etc, due to these cords and most of these cords are soul transferred by leaders Prophets Apostles Pastors Bishops etc, (Meaning an in Ironic way these leaders are Jedi's in the spirit realm and can see your weakness and will prophecy to you in detail what's occurring in your life and you have no clue what spirit is operating or even if it's a familiar spirit or soulish, or yes the gifts are without repentance and the anointing works yes, but how do you know their intention or motive is to transfer there soul into you, yes their astro projection spirit to clone you to what they become! Just like the Disney characters the villains join us we will give you all the Kingdoms of this Earth and everything in it, just like Satan asked Yeshua at the mountain top if you will just Kneel and Bow and Worship me!

About Prophet Anthony Montoya

From a divorced, homeless and hopeless situation, The Lord has anointed Prophet Anthony Montoya and he is mightily being used of The Holy Spirit with an insightful prophetic word designed for you to experience Yahshua's presence and power, break the bonds of demonic influence, deal with stress and give you victory through Yahshua.

Since I'm an ordained minister, my belief is to be a life living sacrifice for Yahweh's kingdom, only to be servant to others and help one another reach Yahweh's purpose and destiny in our lives. To unveil the mysteries and revelations of this kingdom age for all his children to be set free from religion, jezebel spirits, spirit of influence, psychology, false hope (false prophesies), rejection, abandonment guilt, shame, control, seared conscious, subconscious, conscious, mesocratic cells , trauma, familiar spirits, camellia spirits that transforms and changes color, cockatrice spirit, the false god of Prosperity, Fortune & Destiny, mystical influences that general spirits have had dominion over us.

www.ingramcontent.com/pod-product-compliance
Lightning Source LLC
LaVergne TN
LVHW021624080426
835510LV00019B/2745